In **Ultra WURDZ** a certain kind
delights and, I hope, savour this c ·,
vulgar, weird, insults - from mild to sё ،unny,
sometimes bizarre, oddities.

But if you don't enjoy it, you could alwayっ pass the book on to
someone you dislike and say:

'The moment I saw this book, I thought of you'

Ultra WURDZ is a *New Improved*

sequel to the earlier collection below.

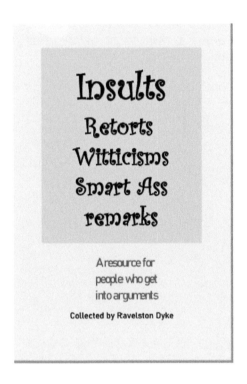

Both books provide ammunition for people who get into arguments, work with words - writers, speakers – or amusement for those who simply enjoy language.

Culled mostly from comments on YouTube.

NOT FOR CHILDREN
or (over) sensitive individuals

ISBN: 9798850968779

www.seviourbooks.com

Disclaimer
Apart a few exceptions, I am not the author of these remarks and I have no record of who is. But if you are and you'd like to be credited, please let me know.

ravelston@seviourbooks.com

Note: Entries are 'as found', some contain words which aren't in any dictionary.

Serving Suggestion

Stuck for a good turn of phrase for your article, book or speech? Open this collection anywhere and browse – the muse will descend and suggest a bon-mot to you.

Contents

Insults

To explain 'stupid' to aliens,
we could begin by describing you.

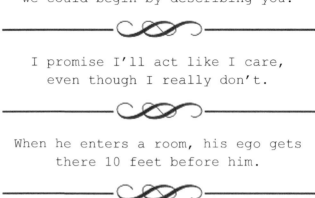

I promise I'll act like I care,
even though I really don't.

When he enters a room, his ego gets
there 10 feet before him.

Please name your source of information so we can
fact-check it. And the dead space between
your ears doesn't count.

I don't want to say 'bitchy' because
that would describe her perfectly.

Conspiracy theory moron says what?

If you are not too busy condescending me.

I'd rather you can think straight
than walk straight.

Grow up flooble you inept gonk.

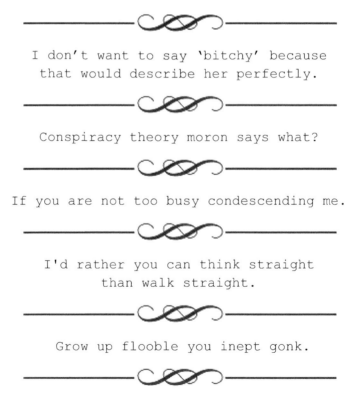

Of course! It all makes sense now.

Now, you promised the Charge Nurse that you would behave yourself today if she let you play on the computer. Behave and curb your childish insults, otherwise it's back into secure unit for the weekend.

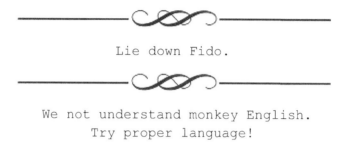

Lie down Fido.

We not understand monkey English.
Try proper language!

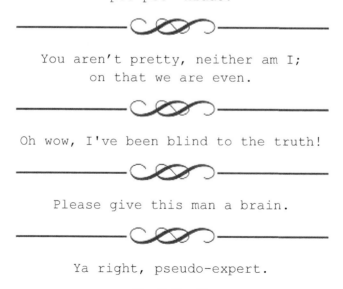

Try to say something more substantial than "Poo poo pee pee" kiddo.

You aren't pretty, neither am I;
on that we are even.

Oh wow, I've been blind to the truth!

Please give this man a brain.

Ya right, pseudo-expert.

Jesus God, read the article/my post/etc) genius.

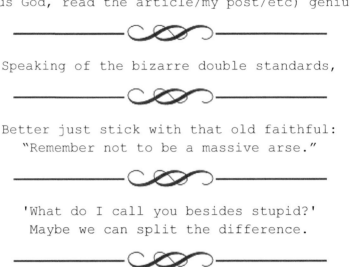

Speaking of the bizarre double standards,

Better just stick with that old faithful:
"Remember not to be a massive arse."

'What do I call you besides stupid?'
Maybe we can split the difference.

I don't give a wet handkerchief.

Are you a mind-reader like so many on here?
Guess how many fingers I´m holding up
right now.

Yours is the view from the window of a rocket
that has long slipped the surly bonds
of reality.

Being fat drunk and stupid is no way
to go through life, son . . .
. . . Being a donkey is no way
to go through life either, dad.

That's right, you're wrong.

I'm SO looking forward to not knowing you.

Absolute dog waste:
I reached for a plastic
bag after I read your remark.

Your day has passed, see you at the cemetery.

I thought of you today,
then I remembered to
take out the trash.

You're trying so hard to be convincing that
[XXX] has been a banquet, when really,
it's a pile of rotting garbage.

Winter's coming for you and your lot.

Your insincere and putrid remark
deserves no response.

You're trying to communicate,
I can tell, bless your heart.

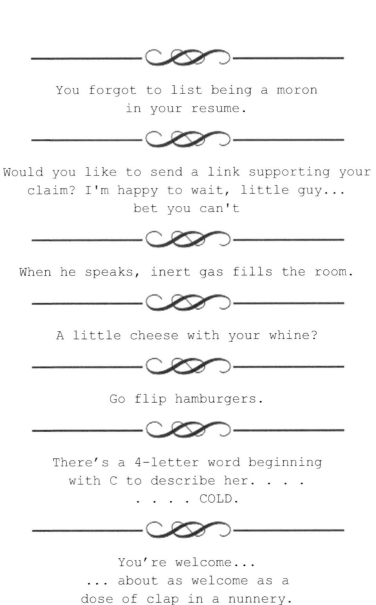

You forgot to list being a moron
in your resume.

Would you like to send a link supporting your
claim? I'm happy to wait, little guy...
bet you can't

When he speaks, inert gas fills the room.

A little cheese with your whine?

Go flip hamburgers.

There's a 4-letter word beginning
with C to describe her. . . .
. . . . COLD.

You're welcome...
... about as welcome as a
dose of clap in a nunnery.

We are waiting for the day
when you don't wake up.

Freeform rambling;
noise devoid of all meaning.

He immatures with age.

Perhaps you should engage your brain
before your fingers.

Do you know who finds you
absolutely fascinating?
... You.

Pull your dress down little man,
your dumbfuckery is showing.

She is as popular as herpes.

It's almost as if you are a hypocrite.

All you lemmings are high on meth.

It appears that the asylum now has Wi-Fi.

Get back in your Petri dish.

Humour not your strong point I'm guessing?
I bet you're fun at parties.

I suspect you're just indulging in a bit of self-
pleasuring with that remark.

Since you are resorting to personal attacks
and not trying to defend your original
argument or add anything else,
I'm going to end this now.

Jabroni, a loser, poser, lame-ass.

I'm not sure who to believe: On the one hand there
are psychologists and behavioural therapists with
solid evidence gained from scientific studies… On
the other hand there is you and your assertions.
Based on the new information you've provided, I'd
happily amend the above point to say '...you, your
assertions and anecdotal evidence'.

Don't let a little knowledge get in
the way of your prejudices.

My cats litter box is filled with things smarter than that piece of shit.Of course, with that I'm insulting things in the litter box.

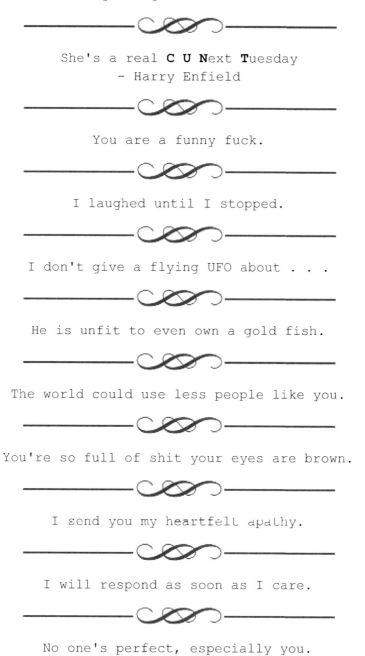

She's a real **C U N**ext Tuesday
- Harry Enfield

You are a funny fuck.

I laughed until I stopped.

I don't give a flying UFO about . . .

He is unfit to even own a gold fish.

The world could use less people like you.

You're so full of shit your eyes are brown.

I send you my heartfelt apathy.

I will respond as soon as I care.

No one's perfect, especially you.

Change the record;
it's as warped as your brain.

She's a beast in human garbage.

It's almost as if you're an unscrupulous
opportunist who blows whichever way
the wind goes.

He tripped and bruised his ego.

Couldn't happen to a nicer piece of shit.

Wake me up before you gogo.

Please, say something half intelligent.

Your sewer-level character.

I'm busy right now, I'll ignore you later.

I am not insulting you;
I am describing you.

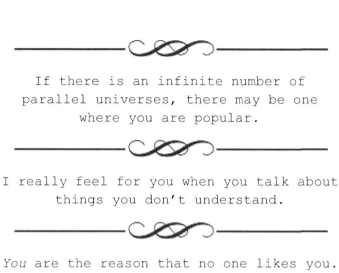

If there is an infinite number of
parallel universes, there may be one
where you are popular.

I really feel for you when you talk about
things you don't understand.

You are the reason that no one likes you.

We regret the vacancy has now been filled.
Suggestion: try MacDonalds.

Your posts are misanthropy
in a négligée of libertarianism.

If you don't want a sarcastic answer,
don't ask me a stupid question.

Please give this man a brain.
What a maroon.

Whatever anecdotal nonsense you choose to
believe so that you can feel better
about your poor health choices,
it won't change science.

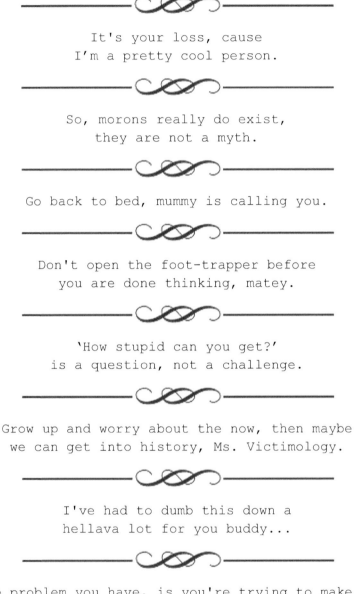

It's your loss, cause
I'm a pretty cool person.

So, morons really do exist,
they are not a myth.

Go back to bed, mummy is calling you.

Don't open the foot-trapper before
you are done thinking, matey.

'How stupid can you get?'
is a question, not a challenge.

Grow up and worry about the now, then maybe
we can get into history, Ms. Victimology.

I've had to dumb this down a
hellava lot for you buddy...

The problem you have, is you're trying to make an
analogy which is not analogous.

It is my duty as a good human

to warn others to avoid you.

That's the stupidest thing
I've read this week.
You really are spezchul.

The difference between ice cream
and your advice:
I asked for the ice cream.

Rank, cliché-ridden, revisionism; a
ready bag of pedestrian sophistry.

Phew! And here's me listening to
those that know.

Read what I wrote again, a little bit slower,
then maybe you'll understand it.

For the love of everything that is good and
holy in this world, desist!

Stop with the pantywaist
politically-correct nonsense.

Could you structure that into a sentence
which can be followed?

Absolutely meaningless without context.

Now get off to school.
Don't forget your packed lunch.

If you answer yes to that question,
how is the weather on Mars?

Just because you are offended,
doesn't mean you are right.

The first step towards
acceptance in psychology is denial.

Sadly some of us don't get beyond that point.

. . . and slip off to the
irrelevance you came from.

I had something else in mind.
* * *
Well keep it there.

Ya right, pseudo-expert.

Objectively false. Look it up.

Do not bandy words with me

Even Puppets have hierarchies...
and Muppets are above them still.

Are you paid well for these juvenile remarks?

Are you through?

Bark up another tree, fascist.

Clearly I rattled your cage;
thank you for displaying your discomfort.

Here's $.50, please go away.

How are things in Jonestown?

How to use flimsy anecdotal evidence
to draw broad conclusions:

'My friends told me,
and I agree,so it must be true'.

How's that working out for you?

Huh? That was as clear as concrete.

I applaud your effort in writing
so much drivel!

I assume you are a liar and traitor?

I do hope your vet treats
your distemper properly.

I miss the good times
when I didn't know you existed.

Just wondering if you were born stupid,
or if you had to work at it.

Oh dear!

Okay. Broken record, I get it.

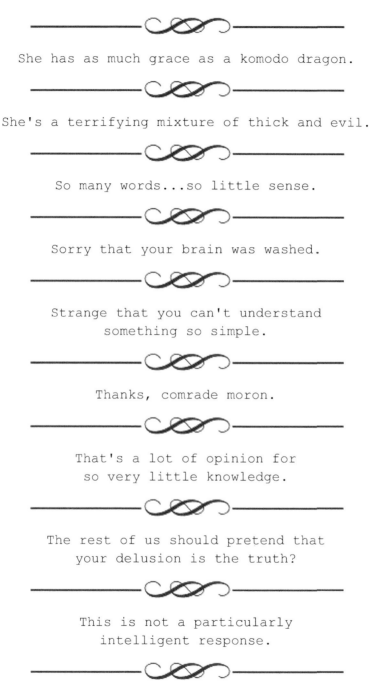

She has as much grace as a komodo dragon.

She's a terrifying mixture of thick and evil.

So many words...so little sense.

Sorry that your brain was washed.

Strange that you can't understand
something so simple.

Thanks, comrade moron.

That's a lot of opinion for
so very little knowledge.

The rest of us should pretend that
your delusion is the truth?

This is not a particularly
intelligent response.

Spotty-faced, sixth form level journalism.

I warn you that trying to impress me
is a waste of time.

Q anon:
Q as in patriot.
U as in idiot.

Don't start with the whataboutism,
aka non sequitur.

Conspiracy theory moron says what?

Could you structure that into a sentence
that can be followed?

Ever thought about a career in comedy?
Don't.

Gravity / sanity has left the chat.

Grow up flooble, you inept gonk.

Hard night wazzit?

I appreciate your deep, meaningful
analysis of the problem.

I get a headache listening to you.
Causation, maybe; correlation, definitely.

I tell you this in a friendly way.

I think the word you're looking for is tw@.

I'd love to hear the logic
behind your statement.

Maybe all these years I've been wrong
but, I highly doubt it.

I'm sorry, I hadn't realised that
you are not very bright.

If my comment sets you off, seek help.

Interesting viewpoint,
not entirely without merit.

It's funny that the bravest talkers say that.

Let go of my leg and get DOWN!

Mummy says not to talk to crazy people.

Not worth the keystrokes to repeat.

One cannot reason with those who
embrace the unreasonable.

Only keyboard warriors know the real truth.

Please get out of the basement and
let mother use her computer.

R U OK, hun?

If English isn't your first language or you have a
learning disability, I won't hold it against you
for not understanding.

Reading comprehension, get some.

Take your remarks to the
slums of The Guardian.

That has to be the dumbest comment in
the history of humanity.

That's a nuthinburger!

The silence was broken by Richard Evan's
effortless ability to miss every point.

They have a term for you: Putin Stroker.

Politics

If democracy means government of the people by the
people and for the people, then it will never
happen while the organs of influence are controlled
by a small number of people whose aims are very
different from those of the masses.

* * *

Wealth buys influence and shapes society to the
benefit of the rich. Minor alterations to taxation
will not change this. It's utopian to think about
a world without people who are hugely more
wealthy than the proletariat, but until this
state comes about, we are stuck with
the Golden Rule: He who has the
gold makes the rules.

Politics is showbiz for ugly people.

Fantasist politicians want to have
their coke and snort it.

Who the f*** failed in art School this time?
(Re: the right-wing extremist plot.)

Fascism is characterized by authoritarian,
dictatorial power; forcible suppression of
opposition; strong regimentation of society
and the economy; and ultra-nationalism.

All you need is a taste for
violence, and a dream!

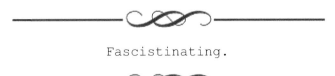

Fascistinating.

If you focus all your energy and resource on
cronyism and getting re-elected, you can make life
much harder for millions of people in a relatively
short space of time.

Politicians usually only turn to memoir writing
when they have accepted that
their race is run.

Poland is praying for rain during a draught and
entrusting the energy network
to Virgin Mary.

Integrity! Yeravinalaff, aintcha?

In a police state the law is not there to protect
you, the citizen, it's there to provide
the ones in power with
a veil of legitimacy.

Laws are for poors!

We will all learn the truth when Trump is back. I only trust people who are pathological liars.

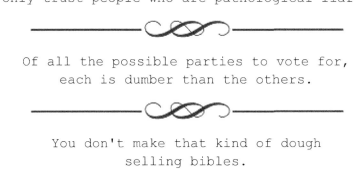

Of all the possible parties to vote for, each is dumber than the others.

You don't make that kind of dough selling bibles.

In a capitalist society, man exploits man, in a socialist one, it's the other way around.

Elections are just window dressing to fool blind morons like you.

I think Putin is going to get at least 110% of all votes.

Free market economy: free from morals.

If you don't have the cash, you can always print it.

It's so easy to gamble with other people's treasure.

'It matters not what form of government Russia has.
Its North Star, world domination,
is a fixed one.'
- Karl Marx

If you must go for the worst possible choice in
this worst possible of all political worlds do
not expect a Panglossian outcome.

Time to start sprinkling the
Reichstag with gasoline.

If you focus all your energy and resource on
cronyism and getting re elected, you can
make life much harder for millions of
people in a relatively short
space of time.

Journalists and newspapers need bogymen
what else would fill the pages?

This privileged priority channel:
the crony express.

The Dreyfus Affair.
The draw of anti-semitism is intimately tied
to national decline; masses of people were

willing to believe conspiracy theories
and target Jewish people, often
violently, when their national
identities were in doubt.

A few decades later a combination of conspiracy
and national anxiety drove Hitler's rise in
Germany.

Crime does not pay
. . . as well as politics

Politicians usually only turn to memoir
writing when they have accepted
that their race is run.

Call this fascism? C'mon you great ponce.

I came across far-right Serbs in Bosnia nearly 30
years ago and if you've got far-right Serbs
supporting you, you're definitely
on the wrong side of history.

We hang the petty thieves and appoint the
great ones to public office.
– Aesop

American Politics

It's a two-party system, Dumb and Dumber.

It helps, in general, not to be American.

The land of the thief, the home of the slave.

A US president with no moral authority
flies in to meet a British prime minister
with no authority whatsoever. Each
seeking legitimacy in the presence of
the other. They hail their special
relationship like two bald men
might brandish a comb.

So campaigns are not about who is the
best candidate for the job, but which
one has the most money to
buy the office.

Who'd have thought?

'Sure beats giving that money to the
poor/needy/marginalized'.

(Re: the Democrats election campaign fund.)

(Vice President) Harris has the IQ of a
cod fish. She couldn't run a 7-11

even less run this country.

I am voting for the man who is
not in Putin's pocket!!

Biden's Yuge advantage is when Fatti
Orange is the GQP nomination.

American nightmare: no matter who
wins in 2024, America loses.

Biden's big advantage, he's sane;
Trump, not so much.

I was really hoping that Flabberino 45
would have had a major stroke
and/or coronary by now.

America is run by big money; they press the idea
that you have some kind of choice. In fact,
your choice is just a different
colour of the same kool-aid.

'We either hang together or we shall
certainly hang separately.'
- Benjamin Franklin

The United States of Zimbabwean America

Canada - like America, but better

Isn't 'Libtard' somewhat derogatory?

Americans are more importanter
than everyone else.

Poor Rudy, all he ever wanted to do is
be corrupt and touch himself.

Free-range Fauci.

Because we were apparently running low on
existential nightmares in 2022, House
Speaker Nancy Pelosi today raised the
risk of war with China by visiting
Taiwan to take in the culture, food
and rich opportunities to cause
international incidents.

We Republicans are on Russia's side.

They should employ some Brits to
Burn the White House again.
We're good at that.

I think we should have trial by combat!'
- Rudy Guiliani.

Jared, like a fucking oligarch, plans to buy up
all the distressed assets created
by the pandemic.

Q. What borders on stupidity?
A. Canada and Mexico.

Kayleigh:
a blank stare, a plastic smile
and a cross around her neck.

Republicans love Putler:
'Putin is awesome! A world hero! A genius!'

Nixon: no longer the worst president.

And so it was that Giuliani was standing in front
of a dozen or so Trump lawn signs taped to the
garage door of a commercial landscaping
company when he learned That the
AP and all the networks
had called the race for
Joe Biden.

USA, a country founded on
ethnic-cleansing and slave labor.

A Crime Against Humanity never troubled Truman, who
drank whiskey, smoked cigars, played poker and
piano, with his buddies at the WH,
while Hiroshima was obliterated,
without warning, in an act of
pure revenge and karmic Evil.

George W. Bush and Dick Cheney go to a restaurant.
The President scans the menu and then asks the
waitress for a 'quickie'. She looks surprised
and says. 'Mr President, I wouldn't have
expected that from you; from
your predecessor, maybe.'

Cheney leans across and whispers to Dubya,
'George, it's pronounced KEESH'.

What a Giuliani you have become!

Trump

The 'playboy' who pays for sex.
The 'patriot' who dodged the draft and
attacks dead Veterans and their widows.
'The genius' who hides his college grades.
The 'Christian' who doesn't go to church.
The 'billionaire who hides his tax returns.
The 'philanthropist' who defrauds charity.
The 'businessman' who bankrupted three
Casinos and lost over $1B in 10 years.

A man of no fixed beliefs other than
in his own right to rule.

You can grab them by the pussy.

When first elected, Trump fit the bill for the
demographic - lost souls looking for a "father-
figure"/messiah to lead them to the promised land,
and out of the morass of their negative existence.
Their lack of education; poor employability
options; alleged oppression by the elites;
inadequate housing; with wealth distinctly
concentrated in areas outside
of their zip codes, etc.

In turn, "DJT noted that "He loved
the poorly educated".

All con-men do.

Trump on his way out; Putin on his way out.
They both thought they ruled the world.

(Thank you for) this / your powerful display of
stable genius / for your
profound ignorance.

I bet 45 would never say: "I believe Putin more
than I do the US Intelligence agencies."
Knowing he was on microphone
on a world stage.

Oh, wait...!

Trump commonly uses this mob-boss-derived method:
He speaks in fluent innuendo and implication,
making his desires clear while leaving himself
just enough vagueness to be able
to smirkingly deny it.

Trump, a sad nobody who sold his soul to
Putin due to some closeted
homoerotic obsession.

Let him try on a pair of those special state-issued
chromium bracelets - no leg irons, he has that
nasty case of draft-dodger-osis in his foot,
so leg irons would be inhumane,
but slap the cuffs on him.
He deserves it.

If anyone on this planet deserves it,
Donald Trump does.

Draft-dodging mobster.

It was miraculous. It was almost no
trick at all, to turn

vice into virtue;
slander into truth,
thievery into honor,
blasphemy into wisdom,
arrogance into humility,
impotence into abstinence,
plunder into philanthropy,
brutality into patriotism,
and sadism into justice.
A nobody could do it.

It merely required no character.

Many believe Trump would not be president without
the right-wing media ecosystem Murdoch created.

We'll see what happens

If I act like Trump, can I
stay out of jail too?

Trump's lawyer is like the dog trainer trying to
teach an old stubborn dog a new trick.
Probably going to end up

biting the trainer.

"Trump Breaks Judge's Rule One Day
into Trial" "Gee, I'm shocked."
Said nobody ever.

It will be shocking if Trump really and truly
suffers a significant consequence. It has never
happened other than losing an election.
And we all saw how well he handled that

His entire company is upside down,
bleeding red ink.

Is there a more blatant example of "contempt
of court"? Throw this entitled
donkey in jail!

If Trump is seeing how far he can go with a
judge, imagine him seeing how far
he could go with a woman.

His cult loves the Tangerine Turdle

The difference between a bean and a chickpea?
Putin doesn't have a tape of Trump
watching a bean.

A spoon full of Clorox helps the
medicine go down - try some.

I'm like a smart person. I know the biggest words,
believe me. I'm a very stable genius?

45's Top Hits:

Pay off
Handcuff
Jail date
Tax return
Best words
Steep ramp
Glass water
Nobody knows
Toilet paper
Strong Covfefe
Person Woman Man Camera TV
Handcuffs jumpsuit prison solitary

You sir, are a genius,
and I say that very strongly.

He just grabs it by the preamble.

There has been one disastrous
Mishap after another.

- Quitting the Paris Agreement,
- Quitting the Iran Deal,
- Moving the US embassy to Jerusalem
- Prompting a massacre,
- And now this North Korea failure.

Trump should just concentrate
on fucking up America.

Another victory notch in Putin's belt.

Trump's qualifications do not extend beyond
the ability to unwrap a cheeseburger.

His conscience is clean –
it's never been used.

What the hell does he think war is, skipping
through a field of daisies singing Kumbaya?

Who lies more, rugs on the floor or DJT?

A sociopath who has the
attention of a goldfish.

41

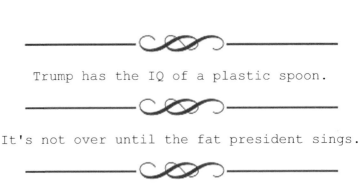

Trump has the IQ of a plastic spoon.

It's not over until the fat president sings.

If you thought that placing an unstable incompetent clown from reality TV into world's most important leadership position would be good for you, you are stupid.

Not just plain stupid, but a special type of stupid; hupid. That's hate + stupid.

The Don is a Lizard. Put him in a large tank and feed him Locusts and on Sundays Cockroaches.

The principal difference between Bannon and Trump is perfume. Both need to be bagged for curbside pickup.

A racist bigot in an obese shell – a hero to the idiots who believed his rhetoric.

An unhinged proto-fascist.

When my Dad started acting like Trump does we took the TV remote away from him, we didn't give him a country to play with!

With each day, however, it's clearer that the secret of Trump's success is cheating. He, and those around him, don't have to be better than their opponents because they're willing to be so much worse.

Trump does a brilliant impression of Alex Baldwin.

Trump is the blueprint for idiots and his appallingly ignorant supporters are the finished products.

Their revoltingly ostentatious Manhattan penthouse, which is decorated in a style best described as Dictator Chic.

A quintessential conman.

Every time he does that, another angel loses its wings.

As we now know, being described in superlatives by Trump almost always marks the subject as an incompetent.

Nambia is such a bigly friend of the US.
We buy a lot of Covfefe from them.

Donald Trump: an ungodly amalgam
Of Juan and Evita Peron.

Trump hasn't touched a drop of alcohol or
mind alerting drugs in his life.

Don't cry for Trump, America. The truth is,
he'll never cry for you.

Melania: the gold digger's gold digger.

The first one-term president in years and the only
one to lose the popular vote twice.

He will be remembered for what he was:
a lying, racist, sexist, misogynist,
colluding slug.

He's not lying,
he's simply expressing sentiments
he knows to be false.

I think I am actually humble. I think I'm much
more humble than you would understand.

Marla Maples - 'Nice tits, no brains',
as he would later sum her up.

'His lack of education is more than compensated
for by his keenly developed moral bankruptcy.'
– Woody Allen

Impeached is forever.

Clorox will erase the evidence.

He shoved his nose up the Flabby Orange Butt,
and enjoyed the toxic aroma.

Do you know how bad you have to be for Paris to
ring church bells when you lose?
And fireworks in London?

We will ALWAYS worship him no matter what THEY say
about facts or what he does wrong Or his silly
lies. We don't care that he's a Narcissistic
sociopath, serial liar, adulterer, draft dodger,
hates our POW soldiers, trusts the Russian
government over our own, discredits
our brave FBI officers, or that he's
obviously not sharpest tool
in the shed...

He's OUR President.

It's the 'Gruesome Trainwreck' factor, but with
an orange haired petulant racist asshole
instead of a train.

Donald is definitely a fright risk.

C'mon man, Trump is releasing his
healthcare plan any day now.

DJT noted that...'he loved the poorly educated'.

'I am deeply in love with Kim Jung Un
and I write him love letters.'

They KGB had collected a lot of information on his
personality so they knew who he was personally.
The feeling was that he was extremely
vulnerable intellectually, and
psychologically, and prone to
flattery, Mr Shvets said.

President Trump referring to the
challenges facing Puerto Rico:
'This is an island, surrounded by
water, big water, ocean water.'

A sad nobody who has sold his soul to Putin due to some closeted homo-erotic obsession.

'He got the way to make the hicks happy.'

Deja coup
(Impeachment #2)

For his birthday he wanted a dictatorship, but he didn't get it.

He wouldn't piss on those people pleading fora pardon if they were on fire.

His actions sealed his fate: out of power, disgraced, devalued beyond repair.

'I love nuclear weapons, no one knows them like I do. We have them, I don't know why we don't use them.'▨
- D J Trump

Name ONE thing he did that was successful. Just one.

I'll wait.

The mould in my fridge deserves more respect than
Trump. He failed at every single thing he tried.
Steaks (he sold 12),ties, water, wine, vodka,
Trump U, the Plaza, the Taj Mahal, Trump
airlines, the MUO, his yacht, 2 marriages.
His buildings only have a 35% tenancy
with 50% of them looking to sell but
can't. Who wants a Trump apt?

Every time he sees he's going to lose money he
files for bankruptcy, 6 in all.
His clubs are in the red too.

No American bank will touch him and Deutsche bank
will cut him off after (if) they collect their
1.8 billion which he doesn't have unless
he can grift it off his followers.

He's already milked 200 million off them.

He will doubtless be described as a consequential
politician,but the consequences are the same
as having a pigeon fly into your kitchen.

Now he will see himself as invincible and the
capitol attack is only the beginning.

Jazz is when the Joker become president.

About Trump's physical appearance now in Mar a
Lago, 'He needs to go up a bra size . . .
and that's just his chin.'

Hydroxy chloroquine, injecting bleach,
shining lights inside the body
and cleaning the lungs.

If imprisoned, don't go for a shower Donny.

Dining with Trump
Menu: cold fast food,
warm Diet Coke.

Mr. Orange is gonna get squeezed.

Person, woman, man, camera, TV . . . impeachment.

It goes up faster than Trumpenstein's orange
monster in a room full of school girls.

The turds don't fall far from Trump's ass.
(ref. Jared / Ivanka.)

He certainly shares traits with fascism the
disdain for elections, the personal cult,

a suggestion of military fetish, etc.

Criticise him for those things all you want. . .
they're disgraceful and worthy of criticism.

He crossed the stage like an alien who's just
read the theory of human movement.

He was in the room where it happened.

Can't wait to see Ivanka in a debate . . .
Will Sarah Palin volunteer to coach her?

Trump: "I want to see Biden in prison!"
Biden: "Why does Trump think I would
visit him in prison?"

There are more troops right now in
Washington DC than in Afghanistan,
said Seth Moulton, a Democratic
lawmaker from Massachusetts. And
they are here to defend us against
the commander in chief , the
President of the United States
and his mob.▨

30 years of state hospitality

Can we make a jail cell that looks like the oval
office, put him in and just tell him
he was reinstated?

First he said there was no cat.

- Then he said he has been assured no cat had
been kicked.

- Then he said if a cat was kicked, he wasn't
there.

- Then he said if he was there, he didn't know
cats were being kicked.

- Then he said he was ambushed by a cat.

- Then, when the photo of him with the cat
appeared, he said, 'Even if I did kick a
cat, I didn't realise that I was kicking
a cat'.

- Then, when the police said he did kick a
cat, he said kicking a cat is like a
parking fine.

- Finally, he paid the fine and said, I
won't resign over a kicked cat.

Hitchin' on that wrecked Trump train.

A lot of people don't realize that playing golf
is an integral part of developing a vaccine.

Let's be honest, we'd all sell Eric off

for a single Dorito chip.

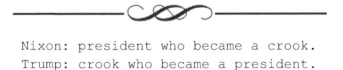

Nixon: president who became a crook.
Trump: crook who became a president.

It didn't help that they looked craven while everything burned. Ivanka and her husband Jared Kushner, have spent the past five years performing a mincing dance around reality, spinning their own parallel universe.

British Politics

Modern Britain: full of liars and lawyers, of
cheats and chancers, of politicians on the make and
on the take,of secret love affairs,
mysterious middlemen and the
perennial temptations of
power, money and sex.

This Tory government spaffed
billions on a Covid response handing
out taxpayers' money to their friends, and
murdered 300 thousand of our own citizens.
This decision exposes local communities to
degradation of their quality of life and well-
being, and trumpets the power of international
investors, working through their lawyers, to work
with impunity against the interests of communities.

Don't judge the country (UK) by your EDL mates in
that flat-roofed pub on your
sink estate flooble.

Drowning is so much cheaper for the Tory
government. (re: refugees in boats)

Starmer, refuses to back them when his duty is
plainly to do so), but he clearly stood by
those in the country's service who are
being cheated of a just wage by
politicians driven by ideological
and corrupt influences.

I remember O'Grady projecting a "hypercompetitive" UK outside the EU. That was obvious code for poverty wages
and lax standards.

The EU called your bluff, and you lost to economorons like Farage and Mogg.

We now have a group of ideologues bent on transforming the UK into a libertarian paradise for the rich and an authoritarian hellhole for everyone else.

Sunak: he's a one dimensional numbers geek with no emotional intelligence.

They reckon the fishermen and farmers will vote Tory no matter what,
because of reasons.

Leavers screwed up the country, destroyed the trust and cooperation with our neighbour and now have absolutely no idea how to put the multiple cats we released back in the bag."

Marriage was broken. UK didn't love EU anymore so there were no a common project for future.

There's no shortage of cheap substandard stuff in this world, and the UK can't compete on that market, no matter how low wages, work conditions, public services, and climate/environment protections fall.

All Tories, gutless lying thieves.

The self-sainted Starmer

What was that dreadful thud?
The sound of Keir Starmer falling off his high horse

Etonians v. Etonians - whadda lark.

I woke up hungry in a cold house and realised, same Tory shit: different day.

I'm voting for Putin in the next UK elections.

Doesn't Blair thinking about.

The sliver of silver lining is that she's

dumb so her shit is hateful and spiteful
but never really effective.
(Re: Priti Patel.)

Jacob Rees Mogg, whose intellect remains
very much single breasted.

Sunak's abstemious diligence offered a
contrast to Johnson's exuberant
shamelessness. He spoke
fluent spreadsheet.

A Poundland Paxman.

The broken shopping trolley school of government.

The common denominator of people in
'Little England / English Nationalist'
pubs is belly size.

The Tories are in a bad way.

Good!

Conservatives, being dragged kicking and screaming
into a better world since the dawn of mankind.

Just think how we gasped in horror at the antics
ofTrump and the damage he was causing; how
We wondered at the stupidity of the US
electorate for having put him in power

Look at us now.

The nation formerly known as 'Great' Britain.

Epithets frequently attached to Dominic Raab have
much the same effect as the words
"former nightclub bouncer".

Post-Brexit Britain - 'Why work hard, pay your
bills when you can just be irresponsible,
receive sympathy and free handouts?'

Brexit

Then

and

Now

Brexit, the gift that keeps on taking.

It was a crazy stew of red meat for the base and red herrings about rules and procedures.

The marriage was broken.
UK didn't love EU anymore.
There was no common project for the future.

Leavers should now be called Cleavers and
Remainers should now be
called Regainers.
I have spoken.

The Brits fell under the spell of typical KBG style
disinformation campaigns to leave the E.U. The
poor deluded isolationist
souls in England just woke up with
a splitting headache and
an itchy rash.

Carry on up the Brexshit.

Bumper sticker: 'Brexit, What Were We Thinking?'

Brexit Britons sit around, tutting and shrugging
into their milky tea as they dunk the soggy
digestives of their

impotence, like eunuchs in
a penis factory.

The stories are good and Preston tells them with
his gift for the kind of wry comedy that
suits English decline.

Brexit was the result of mainly older, low
income, low education, left-behind,
parochial English who have never
been anywhere and do not
like furriners.

It is hard to imagine a more uniquely effective
self-inflicted wound; leavers screwed up the
country, destroyed trust and cooperation
with our neighbours and now
have absolutely no idea how
to put the multiple cats
we released back in
the bag.▱

The EU called your bluff, and you lost
to economorons like Farage and Mogg.
They wanted the UK out of the EU,
for an absurd jingoistic reason -
a completely stupid programme
of infantile nationalism.

It leaves nothing of any value
behind, only destruction.

The government is clueless, hanging on to two quasi-religious shibboleths it cannot shed. In its eyes, the hard Brexit it negotiated is a sacred achievement that can imply only opportunity, not crisis.Its faults cannot be acknowledged.

ANOTHER GREAT BREXIT VICTORY!!!
Europe would like to thank Boris, Nigel and Michael for all their hard work and lies! (Re: new Tesla factory in Germany).

Well done, Leavers you won! Enjoy.

Boris Johnson

A venal malignant chancer as PM with a load of third-raters in his cabinet and the Chumocracy wrought large.

A number of prams have been swiftly emptied of all toys.

Can the conservative MPs please put him out of his misery? It's making me miserable too.

Blathering, blustering, bombastic high-flown, high-sounding, but with little meaning.

Given his history of consistent, self-serving dishonesty, let us hope we have finally seen the back of this thoroughly unworthy man.

"I am not alone in thinking that a witch hunt is underway…". Ah, the favorite turn of phrase of those individuals caught misbehaving.

'I think he honestly believes that it is churlish for us not to regard him as an exception, one who should be free of the network of obligation which binds everyone else,'▯

- Martin Hammond, Boris Johnson's teacher at Eton, in a letter to Johnson's father Stanley.

An Old Etonian and former Bullingdon member forced
to follow the rules that should only apply
to ordinary people.

So sad - what's the country coming to?

A shameless professional liar, who tells the
most enormous lies without any
sign of a conscience.

I am being charitable here.

The spat between Johnson and Cummings calls to mind
the description in *1066 and All That* of the
'Roundheads being right but repulsive' and
the 'Cavaliers as wrong but romantic'.

A would be statesman who has profoundly soiled
himself, staggering about at 23.59 pm with his
trousers round his ankles,trying to
find a cab that will take him.

Boris Johnson just announced some pretty
strong sanctions on Russia.

Sad the proles will be eating fried rat.

Boris Johnson, British Prime Minister 2019 - 2022.
Achievements: got Brexit 'done', bilked the English

electorate, further frayed the fabric of democracy, hastened the demise of the United Kingdom as an entity, operated as a useful idiot while banks and asset strippers carved up what remained of an ailing economy,clung onto power for six months longer than was decent, healthy or defensible.

We know from every unrepentant word he utters that he burns with vengeful resentment.

Bozo the bowel movement is hiding, he is not isolating. He doesn't even know which or what family he has and he cares even less.

Even his limited Del Boy equivalent Latin skills,could not help him resolve this absent knowledge.His teachers warned us, his lecturers let it be known they created a degree syllabus just for him, so he could pass; and, his Tory Newspaper editor employer also, kindly warned us, never employ this lazy privileged Tory excuse as a 'leader'.

Johnson believes his motives to be pure yet his stock in trade is personal advantage and betrayal.

Johnson doesn't have the ability to form a plan. Think of the damage he could do if he had.

Johnson flirted with a rather loutish
kind of climate change denialism.

Johnson has consistently demonstrated
That he is a moral-free zone.

Johnson's burning premiership has collapsed.
There's not much point wasting water on the
flames. Just damp down the neighbouring
properties and move.

Johnson's one consistent principle of his career
has been cakeism, his ardent belief that he alone
should be able to have his cake and eat it.

Britain chose, with its eyes open, to elect a
mendacious, faithless, talentless clown. None of
these things were unknowns in 2019.Johnson (in
PMQs) then did a bit of PR for the Rwandan
tourist board; that country was basically
one big holiday camp.

Johnson embodies the spirit of the modern Tory;
arrogant, self serving, complacent, entitled,
out of touch and uncaring.

Johnson said he was giving up the booze. Instead, he delegated that; he ordered an intern to give up booze. Perhaps he should have kept Dom around to run things while he sleeps off the hangovers.

Johnson's ridiculously graceless resignation speech ran the gamut from pettiness to miscast victimhood 'a sort of Bozzymandias', where the vainglory stood in painfully unfortunate contrast to the fact it was all lying in ruins around him.

Note, he only gibbers using the bottom one whilst the top lip is trained not to move but conceal two goofie teeth. This is part reason why we only hear Etonian guffaw noises and half words, but the main reason is because the brain appears disconnected to the mouth.

In medical term it's having posh palsy impediment. The Tories have mistaken the guffawing mumblings for intelligence.

The prime minister's shoplifter's defence: 'Everyone else is nicking stuff'.

There has never been a more upwardly promoted person taken so far beyond his capabilities. The signs were there for us to see: HIGNFY appearances were a warning. He genuinely asked the panel,

'How many wheels does a quad have?'.

The fact that Johnson is prominent in public life
in a supposedly advanced democracy is a damning
indictment on the UK. He's a lazy, self-obsessed,
deceitful, utterly unprincipled fraud, and
he'sndone more damage to our country than
any other modern PM. May he rot in hell.

PM is a serial sleaze, a habitual liar and a
relentless rule-breaker who knows ethics only
as a county to the east of London.

The most painful punishment for him
would be to lose irrelevance.

How is this rat (Johnson)still running the country.
we must be the laughing stock of the world.
While working people are having to resort
To going to food banks this vile excuse
for a human is bumming money to pay
hundreds of pounds for wallpaper.

I despair for the people who struggle on a
daily basis. While we have this arrogant
narcissist in number ten, things
Will only get worse.

Johnson has kicked the sandcastles down
and that's it.

If this goon can get some minge, then
it's all good for the rest of us.

(Carrie Symonds B. Johnson marriage)

Dark Reflections

'What remains of kisses?
Wounds, however, leave scars.'
– Bertolt Brecht

Alcohol, the only thing I like
about being alive.

Of course at this age, halfway to death, a hangover
needs at least three days to bed in.

'You're a bitter little lady.'
'It's a bitter little world full
of sad surprises.'

– Hollow Triumph (1948) Film-Noir

Only the dead will never see war again.

– Plato

If you must go for the worst possible choice in
this worst possible of all political worlds do not
expect a Panglossian outcome.

I've got a bad feeling about this.

'It always looks darkest
just before it gets totally black.'

– Schulz, creator of Charlie Brown cartoons.

It takes a long time to die of despair.

A mind is a terrible thing to garbage.

If it doesn't kill you,
it scars you for life.

'Life is full of misery, loneliness, and suffering
- and it's all over much too soon.'

- Woody Allen

Hermann Göring explained how easy it is to
mobilize the public to war: 'The people can
always be brought to the bidding of the leaders.
All you have to do is tell them they are
being attacked and denounce the pacifists
for lack of patriotism and exposing
the country to danger.

It works the same way in any country.'

A dying hope.

Non-opening parachute for me please.

When you are dead, you do not know you are dead.
It's only painful & difficult for others.
The same applies when you are stupid.

La vie, ça fini toujours mal.

I remember the date exactly, because
it was Hitler's birthday'

- Woody Allen

There's a little hint of sweetness,
there's a little hint of death.

I asked my friend in North Korea how things
were going. He said he couldn't complain.

People often act out of misperceptions, anger,
despair, insanity, stubbornness, revenge,
pride and/or dogmatic conviction.

Medicins san morales
- Doctors without morals.

I don't like people very much,
not even the people I like.

Chagrin and tonic.

Vodka tastes of regret.

Booze, the old libido liberator

"To what do I attribute my longevity?
Bad luck."
— Quentin Crisp

RIP, Rest In Pieces

The fear porn just keeps coming...
(Re: media coverage)

Joy is but a shadow cast by pain.

Jazz and alcohol: my only reasons to live.

Existence is painful.

Death twitches my ear.

Honest, insightful and deeply, darkly funny.

I am suffused with melancholy.

Do not go gentle into that good night,
Old age should burn and rave at close of day.

- Dylan Thomas

Life is suffering: therefore vodka.

Alcohol: aspirin for the soul

Old, bitter and single.

In the desert of pain, joy is a shimmering mirage.

Sleep is Death's brother.

Is there any clearer demonstration of the
futility of human existence than
men watching cricket?

Maxwell

The picture of Bob Maxwell that
emerges is vivid but familiar:
bombastic, florid, devious,
gluttonous, bullying, absurd.

Clive James, spotting Maxwell at
the Cannes film festival,

'He looked like a ton and a half of
half- cured ham wrapped in a white tuxedo'.

Maxwell was a man without friends;
sycophants were a different matter.

When he died, there were
no friends to
miss him,

creditors maybe.

'His size alone made him hard to ignore,
22 stone in the lean years'.

The stink of his family is nearly
impossible to wash off.
(Both Maxwell and Trump)

The perpetrators (or should I say customers?)
aren't being held accountable. They are
neither named nor punished and can

continue undetected.

Re:Epstein/Ghislaine Maxwell sex trafficking

Reply: Two ex-presidents - Bill Clinton and Donald Trump are on that list of customers. Why do you think nobody is held accountable?

Putin / Russia

The bizarro Russian mir!

A war criminal, a fascist and a dictator walk
into a bar. The barman asks
'What'll it be Mr. Putin?'

'I'm worried about the snow being
hurt in this video.'

(Re: battle in Ukraine)

'Emperor Xi Jinping paid a royal visit to Pu Tin,
regional governor of the northern
Chinese province of Ruxia.'
- Garry Kasparov

Most of Russia's stored tanks are
nothing but rust on tracks.

Russia's nuclear arsenal scares me; it's
like a monkey with a machine gun.

Q. Ivan, what is the Russian world?

A. The Russian world is when you live in poverty,
without rights, you can't do anything about it
and don't want to be able to, but you want
to teach this to the whole world.

One day a Russian will say something
that makes sense. I'm sure of it.

Russians are to believe contradictory gobbets of
nonsense and how deeply they are inspired by
Russian nationalism and a sense that they are the
centre of the Universe

"Some of you may die, but it's a sacrifice that
I'm willing to make."

- Putin

If Russian KIA are recovered pensions are issued to
families. Non-recovered are deemed missing,
so no pension is paid.

It's cheaper.

Putin went to a soothsayer to find out what lay
ahead for him in his life. "You will be driven
through Moscow streets filled with people
rejoicing and clapping as you pass",
she told him.

"Sounds good," Putin replied.
"Will I be waving to the crowd?"
"No", the soothsayer replied.
"Your coffin will be closed".

The open windows in Russia are going to
be very, busy this week

Russian worker: "we pretend to work...
they pretend to pay us".

You can't tell something is true for sure
until the Kremlin denies it..."

"We're really turning out to be the occupiers...."
No shit Sherlock - yes, you are!
Tomorrow, you'll find out that water is wet!

A Russian soldier always burns twice:
first in their tanks and trenches,
and after that in Hell.

Russia is now China's appendix, ever
fearful of appendectomy.

Russia is a reckless power and worldwide
humiliation might just be the thing that forces
them to re-evaluate and
think before they act.

The Russian grunts are just a bunch of poor
people who don't have a clue and ate a
bucket load of lies about this
conflict for breakfast.

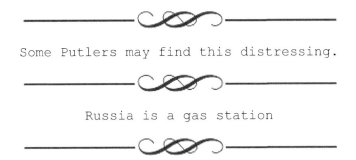

Some Putlers may find this distressing.

Russia is a gas station

'I took my feet in my hands and kept on running'
- Russian POW

It's become obvious the Russian military is
nothing but painted-over rust.

The main problem with cannon fodder is
their incessant whining.

I like my orc medium-rare, these were
obviously way overcooked

The end result will be a worn down and neutered
peaceful country that will leave its
neighbours alone.

I strongly contest your accusation of lack of
professionalism.The Russian military
personnel are top experts in
logistical transfers and sales,
cleaning out the military
black market sales.

A high velocity case of lead poisoning
would solve this problem.

The general, accusing combat veterans of cowardice,
shows a complete lack of how to motivate and
inspire the soldiers under his command.
Personally, I wouldn't follow this guy
to the latrines, much less
than to combat.

Cry me a river you drunk, inbred fascists.
Can't wait to see Moscow burn to the ground.

The residents of Belgorod voted 107.3%
For the annexation.

Are you sure about that percentage? I read that it
was a 103% turnout and 110% voted
to be annexed by Ukraine.

I got this from a reliable source within Russia.
They had dead people vote to get above 100%

What, are you discriminating against dead people?
Next you'll say that unborn have no rights,
discrimination just never ends.

Glorious Russian math make most sense.

As Stalin used to say when asked about the show
trials, torture and executions: 'When you
chop wood, the splinters fly.'

And don't forget Prigozhin stating how the
Kremlin's claims of severe Ukrainian casualties in
recent clashes was wild fiction. But then, you're
not here to be honest, are you?

Are you trying to say that you CAN'T pause
real war for a snack break? Why does
anyone play then?

* * *

Well, you can, as long as every player
knows the rules.

"What matters is not peoples' votes,
but who counts them".

- Stalin.

Putin's coffee went cold in Kiev!
Slava Ukraini!

It's almost like they never should've invaded.

Why don't they lob bottles of
vodka into the trenches?

Doesn't have to be the good stuff.

I can watch these videos (of Russian defeats all
day long until the cows come home, and
even after the cows come home.

The worst war crime a head of state can commit;
the one not even the most hollowed soul
bastard is capable of; one this world
will never forgive, is losing.

More land.
Russia has not enough of it yet.
They need more.

For me it would be just fine if they took their
miserable country and moved to another planet.

One minute you're planning your next dishwasher
heist... the next moment you're dead... how
fleeting the Russian life be.

You have got admire the irony in Putin's speech.
"...Ukraine troops haven't achieved
what they wanted..."

Who am I to disagree, Putin is an expert
on not achieving what he wanted!

On one hand I don't know who blew up the bridge, but on the other foot I have a Nike.

Russia has been given a lifetime supply of trump water, he takes care of his friends.

So after "liberating" these areas they have also made them uninhabitable. Russia, where Tactics from the 13th century are new again!

It is surprising how much damage an apparently small explosive can do when dropped near to the russ.

Did I say surprising? Sorry, I meant good.

Putin: 'Oi, my offensive has NOT 'petered out'.If anything, it's petering up. It's about to hit maximum Peter!'

Lots of oven-ready Orcs in those vehicles. (After a massive explosion)

'A day without tank-fried Orcs is a day wasted'

- V. Zelenskiy.

Russia is Africa with snow.

I tell you this in a friendly way.

Some Putlers may find this distressing.

"A day without tank-fried Orc is a day wasted"
- Chef Zelensky.

One day a Russian will say something that makes
sense.
I'm sure of it.

Competency: the hallmark of the
Russian military!

Living outside of Russia is much better than
becoming a single-use mobik.

Barbecued Orc's....yummy......

Religion

'If God exists, I hope he has a good excuse.'

- Woody Allen

Drink ye and be drunken and spue
and fall and rise no more.

Jeremiah 25:27

Charm is deceitful and beauty passing.

- Proverbs 31:30

Who can find a virtuous woman?
For her price is far above rubies.

- Proverbs 31:10

God fearing as a New York cockroach

Si vousparlez à Dieu, vous êtes croyant.
S'il vous répond, vous êtes schizophrène.

Fortunately, science, and now the ease by which
information travels, mean that there are
fewer dark corners where manipulators
can get away with the deception
which forms the core
of religion.

Jésus changeaitl'eau en vin. Pas étonnant
que douze mecs le suivaient partout.

I went to Lourdes with my wife.
No miracle occurred
- we returned home together.

'In the beginning, there was nothing. And God said,
'Let there be light.' And there was light.
There was still nothing, but you
could see it a lot better.'

- Woody Allen

'Faith' is a term with no application for
a person who has a scientific education.

Deception forms the core of religion.

There is no god, just a cold uncaring universe.
We all end up dead and forgotten.

Go to heaven for the climate, hell for the company.

Religion is regarded by the common people
as true, by the wise as false, and
by the rulers as useful.

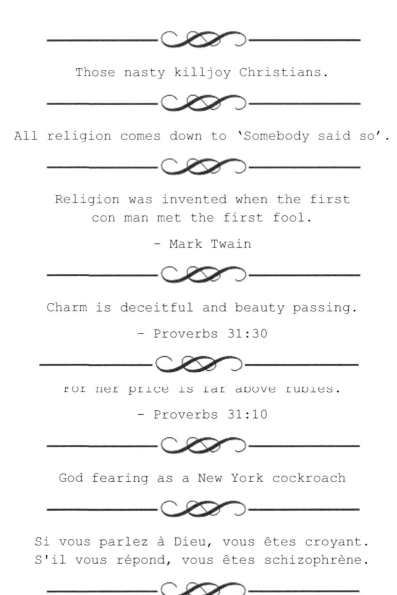

Those nasty killjoy Christians.

All religion comes down to 'Somebody said so'.

Religion was invented when the first
con man met the first fool.

- Mark Twain

Charm is deceitful and beauty passing.

- Proverbs 31:30

for her price is far above rubies.

- Proverbs 31:10

God fearing as a New York cockroach

Si vous parlez à Dieu, vous êtes croyant.
S'il vous répond, vous êtes schizophrène.

Fortunately, science, and now the ease by which
information travels, mean that there are
fewer dark corners where manipulators
can get away with the deception
which forms the core
of religion.

Jésus changeaitl'eau en vin. Pas étonnant
que douze mecs le suivaient partout.

I went to Lourdes with my wife. No miracle occurred
- we returned home together.

If Christianity is on the decline then surely
Christmas's days are numbered? I'm almost sobbing
into my Baileys at the very thought.

The best support I have found for
theexistence of a god:

'Show me the man who can make a dandelion.'

'Faith' is a term with no application for a person
who has a scientific education.

Religion is poison because it asks us to give up
our most precious faculty, which is reason
and to believe things without evidence.

- Christopher Hitchens

Deception forms the core of religion.

There is no god, just a cold uncaring universe.
We all end up dead and forgotten.

'Religion is the impotence of the human mind to
deal with occurrences it cannot understand.'

– Karl Marx

Go to heaven for the climate,
hell for the company.

Religion is regarded by the common people
as true, by the wise as false, and
by the rulers as useful.

Those nasty killjoy Christians.

All religion comes down to
'Somebody said so'.

Religion was invented when the first
con man met the first fool.

– Mark Twain

So Appalling

Putting the dick in dictator.

Time to stop fucking the dog
- I have to get some work done.

It's raining shit and we've got no brollies.

Reverse Midas touch.
I think you mean
the Fecal touch.

He shoved his nose up the Flabby Orange Butt,
and enjoyed the toxic aroma.

Semi-solid oral sewage.

Coffee tastes better if the latrines are dug
downstream from an encampment.

Stick your b*llsh!t where it came from.
'They're all pink on the inside'

- Phil, of the antiques shop.

The leader of his own bowel movements.

I went to see my doctor because I wanted to
give up smoking. She said I would
have to stop masturbating.
I asked why and she said
it made it difficult for
her to examine me.

What's the world come to if you can't
trust a murdering despot?

'Did you see my ratings with the Jews?
I'm so popular!'

– Hitler

"I shat everywhere in my house last night it was
absolutely fucking violent disgusting"

– Socrates

Reply: Stop spreading fake quotes. Socrates never
said anything like that, Diogenes did.

Cupid stunt

"Losers always whine, winners go home
and #&%$ the prom queen"

– Sean Connery in the The Rock 1996

Go suck a pitcher of dicks.

My fist: your vagina.

Here's wishing you a lingering, demoralising death
like cancer, years in and out of hospital, no
breath, rotten teeth, amputations.

Think about it like this, if you get into
trouble as an adult, would you say,
'At least I'm not shitting my pants'?

Everything's a toilet if you're brave enough.

Fuck them and the horse they rode in on.

Q: What are you thinking about?
A: I just hope no one ever finds the body.

I farted.
That's as close as you are
going to get to me giving a shit.

Darling that was not a fart.
I just blew you a kiss from my bottom.

Royalty

Charles: A man who is said to have his shoelaces ironed and his toothpaste squeezed by his valet.

A man whose future has been coming for so long that it's very nearly behind him.

Someone who travels with his own toilet seat.

Andrew will claim not to know Ghislaine Maxwell at all. He's England's top expert in the field of selective amnesia.

Andrew will remain in disgrace until death, while even Charles might have to shuffle off into exile if things turn torrid.

Prince Andrew is in the dogfight of his life, and will now say absolutely anything to prevail in it.

Biologically incapable of sweating biologically incapable of having the first or faintest clue.

– Prince Andrew

I haven't had the worst luck in the world. I've never met Fergie: I hope to maintain that satisfactory status.'▯

Labour said it was 'corruption plain and simple' if Lord Brownlow had access to senior ministers because he was paying for wallpaper.

The status of Britain is similar to that of Puerto Rico; self-governing, but foreign policy is decided in Washington.

If you do not remove incompetence it rises up the chain of command. It's like blood poisoning. The UK is Septicaemia City now.

There's more than one gravy train! Make sure you get onboard. The next one! Hs2 connects to Gravytown.

Prince Charles interviewed on the David Letterman Show: 'Since I'm the only one here without an accent, I'll speak slowly.'

The highbrow travelling circus known as the British royal family.

I don't think anyone's interested in the Ukraine any more. So bomby, so dirty. Can we have something uplifting and newsworthy instead, say more articles on Harry and Meghan?

Oddments

Foam-flecked rage.

'You're breaking my heart, Jack.'
- Phillip Marlowe/Raymond chandler,
In 'The High Window'

Let's just blame china.

Maybe in a vacuum, but not here on earth.

A thundering herd of defenseless souls.

'The dark web ... because it's Black Friday.'

You have unknowingly created a paradoxical
state where the universe cannot resolve
and collapses in on itself due to
impossibility and self-induced
instability of space time.

No wonder he's running around, agitated.
The house is infested with bed rats.

These strange days.

I haven't had steak since breakfast.

Want some pork scratchings to go with that?

If we give money to the poor,
they'll only spend it.

And if my grandmother had wheels
she would be a bicycle.

If my aunt had balls, she'd be my uncle.

How's your wife?'
'Compared to what?'

- Henny Youngman

According to a recent survey, English can be fun.

Low rent Fascism

Nothing unites the people of Earth
like a threat from Mars.

I liked that more than I should.

Many people actually think war is a lot of fun.

This is the act of a responsible idiot.

A knife fight in a phone booth.

That was yesterday's experts.

Definitely a point that should be
discussed with more attention.

The Narcissist's Prayer:

That didn't happen.
And if it did, it wasn't that bad.
And if it was, that's not a big deal.
And if it is, that's not my fault.
And if it was, I didn't mean it.
And if I did, you deserved it!

I don't know what adverbs, conjunctions,
prepositions, interjections, or past participles
are, but I can still talk pretty goodly.
Or so I've been told...

They cling to guns or religion or antipathy

to people who aren't like them'.

Nothing is ever truly laid to rest in science.

We are grabbers. We are scratchers.

You're looking for something that does not, has
not, will not, might not or must not exist,
but you're always welcome to
search for it.

As any bookmaker or bogus Bhagwant can confirm,
there's always money in selling daydreams to
losers. It's certainly easier than
working for a living.

I miss Garrison Keillor.
So does sanity.

'Advertising is the art of convincing
people to spend money they don't have
for something they don't need.'

– Will Rogers

If an anonymous comment goes unread,
is it still irritating?

The stone age didn't end because
there weren't any rocks left.

Quitting smoking is easy,
I've done it hundreds of times.

Where do we go from here? Mars?

African children could have eaten them fireworks.

I measure my coffee intake in
units of the LD 50.

This is rapidly turning into one
of the worst ideas I have ever had
(there are other strong contenders).

L'alcool tue mais combien sont nés grâce à lui?

What is the sound of no hands texting?

'Her smile became a little mechanical'

- PG Wodehouse, The Man Upstairs.

Un égoïste, c'est quelqu'un qui
ne pensé pas à moi.

Ugliness: the most effective contraceptive.

Confidence is what you have before
you understand the problem.

– Woody Allen

Talent is cheaper than table salt.

– Stephen King

'Give me a small bottle of vodka.
That one, the £4.50. How much is it?'
'Five pounds please mate.'

Switzerland on average is flat.

It's high time we got back to small amounts
of corruption and incompetence
in our political leaders.

We're out of the real thing,
but there's some instant covfefe.

In other news:
water, still wet.

I've already done one of those things ....
. . . . and the other one.

Some assembly may be required.

They're gonna use me as an escape goat.

Fairy kisses and rainbows.

A gilded celebrity.

Cloudy, with a chance of meatballs.

Beer: not just for breakfast.

Funny Oddities

Bees visit flowers. If they didn't you'd have
nothing to eat. (Justifying men having affairs).

I took an online IQ test, and scoring 130,
it told me I am in the top two per cent.

'So did I' says Lauren.
Her friend tells her later,
'My dog could score 130 on that test'.

The wheels are coming off the/your submarine.

Who among us hasn't made that mistake . . .
. . . yesterday?

Like Vincent Van Gogh, I will never live to know
how much my work will be loved and admired by
future generations.

A grey moribund carbuncle on the
arse-end of Scotland.

(Originally referring to the town of Forth,
South Lanarkshire, Scotland. There were
many contenders for this title.
(Google it.)

Arbroath is described as a
'mixture of racists and junkies'.
Ballinger in Fife, Scotland, dubbed

'immune to any form of improvement'.

Seed dispersal - how I spent my teen years.

You could kill two birds with
half a dozen bricks.

The writer's breakfast:
coffee and a synonym roll.

The rest is hysterics.

How come fire sauce isn't made with real fire?

The pub was the focal point of community life .For
some, alcohol encouraged joyful moments,
an emigration of the soul from
sometimes unhappy realities.

But for most people the pub was there for sheer
delight.
You never knew who you'd meet, nor what
strange wisdom someone might pass on.

Ideas rebounded from the tobacco-stained walls into
every snug and cranny; giddy fiddles and
rattling tongues could enliven the
darkest corners.

(XXX) will be revealed in all its ignomy.
(ignominy)

To know me is to love me.

First, . . .(this) . Now . . . (that),
I want a new planet!

Everything I write and say is true, be quiet.

That's just what they want you to believe!

I can confirm that 100% of wind turbine accidents
occur because of wind turbines.

It is still true what Voltaire said so long ago . .
. . . but did Voltaire ever envisage
a deep-fried Mars Bar?

'Foolish', you calling me 'foolish'?

Funny

Hard work may not kill you,
but why chance it?

I make new mistakes to cover my old mistakes.

I think America is just being selfish. It should
donate aircraft carriers in a land war.
Can't be too hard to add wheels.

Have you ever noticed how, when all the trees get
together and wiggle their limbs, it gets windy?

A land with no graveyards
is a country of cannibals.

Not knowing what Armageddon means
is not the end of the world.

Pubs are very educational,
full of experts on any
subject you like.

The early bird might get the worm,
but the second mouse gets the cheese.

His baroque private life.

You'll never be as lazy as
whoever named the fireplace.

I don't care if I'm a moron;
at least I'm a moron with standards.

My ignorance is as valid as your knowledge.

It's a dog eat dog world,
and I will eat your dog.

Everyone laughed when I told them I wanted to be a
comedian; well they're not laughing now.

The difference between ignorance and apathy?
I don't know and I don't care.

Dogs can analyse trajectories to intercept flying
objects, but they're crap at explaining physics.

Grammar
The difference between knowing your sh!t

and knowing you're sh!t.

Bees - natural enemy of
the tightrope walker.

I resemble your implication.

A man with hearing problems goes to the doctor
Dr. 'Can you describe the symptoms to me?'

'Yes. Homer is a fat yellow lazy bastard and
Marge is a skinny bird with big blue hair'

Don't blame me for your lack of incompetence.

I mean it with all the confidence
born of ignorance.

In **italics**, cause he's Italian.

I have two bad habits - smoking and masturbation.
I'm a thirty a day man, and I smoke
like a chimney.

German children are kinder.

Free violin, no strings attached.

'A nickel ain't worth a dime anymore'

- Yogi Berra

It is said that one of the hardest things in life
is to stop loving a girl who no longer loves you.
I think that stuffing toothpaste back inside
the tube is even harder.

I accidentally said hello to a feminist
the other day. My trial begins Monday

Thank you for remaining clam.

I mean, who among us can honestly
say they never rode their motorcycle
into a brothel asking for coffee?

- C-Milk

I spent a lot of money on booze, birds and fast
cars. The rest I just squandered.

- George Best

I started out with nothing,
and still have most of it.

I used to go missing a lot...
Miss Canada, Miss United Kingdom, Miss World.

- George Best

Football greats
Pelé - good
Maradona - great
But George Best

I've stopped drinking,
but only while I'm asleep.

I left school in ninth grade to help
mother sell crystal meth.
. . good meth though.

I threw a boomerang once
and now live in perpetual fear.

'I was so poor growing up, if I wasn't a boy,
I'd have had nothing to play with.'
- Rodney Dangerfield

I went to see Walt Disney on ice
but it's just an old guy in a freezer.

'It's one or two hookers and some blow,
I wouldn't necessarily call it partying.'

I keep a bottle of poison on a kitchen shelf
just for emergencies.

We're not in some dark godless void
on the outer edges of human misery?
No, we're in Nottingham.
Same thing.

- Ade Edmondson to Rik Mayall

'If I still had all the money I've spent on drink
over the years, I could spend it on drink'.

- Viv Stanshall as Sir Henry Rawlinson.

'I'm such a good lover because
I practice a lot on my own.'

- Woody Allen

The Irish situation:
they say it's not as bad
as they say it is.

It's better to have loved a short man
than never to have loved at all.

(say it fast out loud)

- Miles Kingston

(Try it also with 'I chased a bug around a tree'.)

The weather will be cold;
there are two reasons for this;
one is that the temperature will be lower.

Herr Kutt, German barber.

What's the French for entrepreneur?

I was caught delicto flamenco.

For all intensive purposes she's illiterate.
The man cannot read or write, he's illiteral.

Two cannibals are eating a clown, one says to
the other, 'Does this taste funny to you?'

I asked for a book about a man who was
sent to Alcatraz but got away.

'You're studying the prison system?'
'No, it's just escapism.'

If a man says he will do something,
he will do it. It is not necessary
to remind him every six months.

- Bill Murray

If you kill a killer,
the total number of killers
remains the same.

Dyslexic guy walks into a bra...

'Knock, knock'
'Who's there?'
'To'.
'To, who'?
'Surely you mean to whom?'

'If we don't succeed,
we run the risk of failure.'

- Dan Quayle

This is the earliest I've ever been late.

'What is the robbing of a bank compared to
the founding of a bank?

- Bertolt Brecht

Advertising is the art of convincing people to
spend money they don't have for
something they don't need.

- Will Rogers

"It's Time To Kick Ass And Chew Bubblegum.
And I'm All Out Of Gum."

- Duke Nukem

I failed exams in some subjects, but my friend
passed in all. Now he is an
engineer in Microsoft and
I own Microsoft.

- Bill Gates

I was born with a plastic spoon in my mouth.

When I use a word,' Humpty Dumpty said in rather a
scornful tone, 'it means just what I choose it
to mean — neither more nor less.'

The drug pusher's argument: if it's not
our coal, it will be someone else's.

If I had asked people what they wanted,
they would have said faster horses.

- Henry Ford

I was worried this would end with me getting
a belly button piercing and
moving to Brighton.

I don't like people very much,
not even the people I like.

Jeez Louise. Is it that difficult to call someone
what they want to be called. If you can call a
man who's not a fried potato, Chip, or a man
who doesn't tighten a drill bit, Chuck,
you can call anyone what they want to
be called without having an
existential meltdown.

My cardiologist told me to get my affairs in
order and gave me about 6 months to live.

I changed cardiologist.

My manager told me something that has
stuck with me for 20 years now:
"No good deed goes unpunished".

My wife majored at sarcasm at Vasa.

Weird

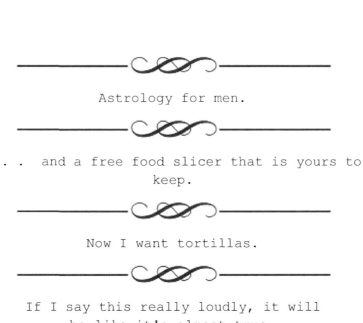

Astrology for men.

. . . and a free food slicer that is yours to
keep.

Now I want tortillas.

If I say this really loudly, it will
be like it's almost true.

Not gonna lie.

One of the regulars gives me a nod
to acknowledge my presence.
I am an 'irregular'
in his pub.

(The Ship, Bristol, UK)

That wheelie bin was only
3 days away from retirement.

The only ones who can
'talk him down from the ledge'.

An esturial oik.

And THAT, boys and girls, is why . . .

The people who deal with the Queen's dog licences.

The algorithm giveth
and the algorithm taketh.

The area's being gentrified within
an inch of its life.

Out of the frying pan, into the
heat death of the universe.

'Badly decomposed body found in
derelict East London pub'

Kraftfahrzeughaftpflichtversicherung:

officially recognised by the Duden, Germany's
pre-eminent dictionary, as the longest word
in the German language.

The 36 letters of the word form a composite,
tongue-tying way to say:

obligatory-motor-vehicle-liability-insurance.

And in a galaxy far, far away . . .

Hey c'mon, you all know what that modern technology
is like. You text a guy for a hundred large,
get a new phone, and forget
that you had asked.

A kaleidoscopic mixture of history, etymology,
diaries, autobiography, fan letters, essays,
parallel lives, party lists, charts,
interviews, announcements and stories.
One Two Three Four joyfully
echoes the frenetic hurly
burly of an era.

Be honest, who is going to care
Other than Gary Neville's mum?

14 different labias which can be
detached and put in the dishwasher.

– ad for sex doll.

As a maid who cleans toilets, I can
say something went wrong.

As a professional dishwasher I can

confirm that something failed here.

Capitalism: freedom to buy all kinds of crap you don't need, with money you don't have, to impress people you don't like.

Fact: our whole planet is in the middle of nowhere. Funny, ain't it?

The Archbishop of Canterbury, the Right Reverend Sunflower Ice-Lolly Jones.

Inspecting the yield of his latest nasal investigation.

'Every gun that is made, every warship launched, every rocket fired signifies, in the final sense, a theft from those who hunger and are not fed, those who are cold and are not clothed. This world in arms is not spending money alone. It is spending the sweat of its laborers, the genius of its scientists, the hopes of its children.'
- US President Eisenhower

They probably won't be able to throw lasers from their fingers but they might be able to throw the fingers...

I like when the electrons get too cold they
just wanna huddle together.

It's like that time I was Captain of the Titanic.

Wise

As a species, we are attached to the self,
to the ideas and practices of the ego:
accumulation, greed, envy, desire,
hatred, anger, fear, conquest.

Charm is deceptive and beauty fleeting

- Proverbs 31:30

Always trust your instincts over your thoughts.
Your thoughts are based on what you have
learned in your life time. Your
instincts were acquired over
millions of years.

They will inform you of your situation instantly.

We think so highly of ourselves, and yet, we are no
more than ego stretched around frail flesh
and knifey calcium.

'Money can't buy you love'.
But love doesn't buy you
anything at all.

Starve a thief and see what he does,
I dare ya.

'Do not be afraid of death
so much as an inadequate life.'

- Bertolt Brecht

Truth left the building a long time ago.

Not even the smartest human has ever been able to
make a dandelion.

Hell is about seeing the
stupid stuff you did.

The dictatorial hunger for
power is insatiable.

The cynic: an optimist with experience.

What brutal creatures we are.
Flees arguing over who owns the dog.

A tragic homage, from one old,
dying white guy, to another.

This isn't negative thinking, it's positive.
You didn't ask to be born, but here you are.
Make the most of this flash of lightning
in the endless dark. Enjoy yourself.
Smoke a cigarette. Eat a fried egg.
Jump out of an airplane.

The greatest failing of the human species is the desire to be led by the most thuggish narcissist/ psychopath available.

Like all systems the intrinsic contradictions begin to show as fault lines.

Love is not always a bad thing.

Presumed guilty until proven innocent.

A spoonful of nonsense helps
the fascism go down.

What's the difference if we're looking at
an eternity of complete and utter
nothingness and oblivion?

Where be your gibes now?
Your gambols? Your songs? Your flashes of merriment
that were wont to set the table on a roar?
Prithee, Horatio, tell me one thing.

- W. Shakespeare, Hamlet

Your lifestyle determines your deathstyle.

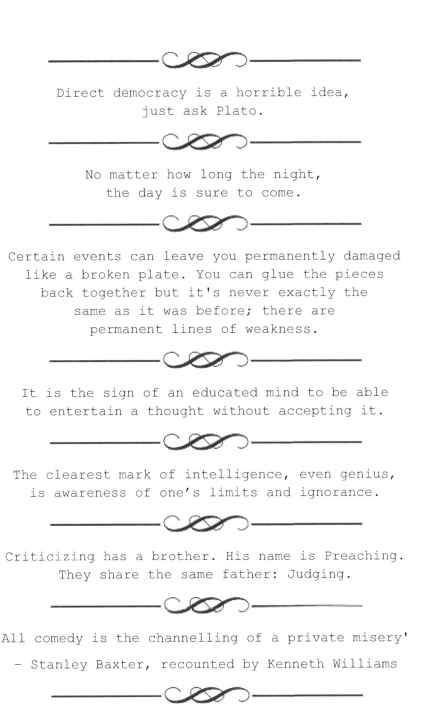

Direct democracy is a horrible idea,
just ask Plato.

No matter how long the night,
the day is sure to come.

Certain events can leave you permanently damaged
like a broken plate. You can glue the pieces
back together but it's never exactly the
same as it was before; there are
permanent lines of weakness.

It is the sign of an educated mind to be able
to entertain a thought without accepting it.

The clearest mark of intelligence, even genius,
is awareness of one's limits and ignorance.

Criticizing has a brother. His name is Preaching.
They share the same father: Judging.

All comedy is the channelling of a private misery'

- Stanley Baxter, recounted by Kenneth Williams

All justifications are just a smokescreen

for personal preferences.

A serial killer could have been thinking of
rainbows and unicorns when they
murdered their victims.

If nobody likes your selfie,
what is the value of the self?

Dans toutes les larmes s'attarde un espoir.

Without ugly, there can be no beautiful.

Karma, it's your move.

Il n'y a pas de comique en dehors
de ce qui estproprement humain.

Life is too short for false friends
and mediocre wine.

Time makes fools of us all in the end.

We either hang together or we shall
certainly hang separately.'

- Benjamin Franklin

'All I know is that I really don't
know anything at all.'

- Albert Einstein.

'It's easier to fool people than to convince them
that they're being fooled.'

- Mark Twain

'Just because your voice reaches halfway
around the world doesn't mean you
are wiser than when it reached
only to the end of the bar.'

- Edward R. Murrow

Men never do evil so completely and cheerfully
as when they do it from
religious conviction.

- Blaise Pascal

No amount of anxiety makes any difference to
anything that is going to happen.

- Alan Watts

No man ever steps in the same river twice,
for it's not the same river and

he's not the same man.

- Heraclitus

A certain darkness is needed to see the stars.

Hatred is a way of life.

Karma: you get what you deserve.

No rain: no flowers.

One day you're the statue.
One day you're the pigeon.

The cost of a single destroyer: new homes
for more than 8,000 people.

* * *

The cost of a single fighter plane:
Half a million bushels of wheat.

* * *

The cost of one modern heavy bomber:
a modern brick school in more than 30 cities;
two electric power plants, each serving
a town of 60,000 population; two
fully equipped hospitals or 50
miles of concrete highway.

The final star in the final galaxy could
quietly burn out, ushering in the
heat death of the universe, and
we still wouldn't be done.

An old mantra: 'Confident,
Cocky, Lazy, Dead'.

Money doesn't buy brain.

That yawning gap between spreadsheet and reality.

There are two things authoritarians cannot handle;
humour and disagreement.

Some people may hate the west, hate America, but as
a Nicaraguan refugee who lived in a country
influenced by Russia, I am more than happy
that it's America & the west & not
theocratic extremist Middle
Easterners,theocratic lunatic
Saudi Arabia, totalitarian
Russia or totalitarian China
who wields the most
influence & power.

Language is no more than

sophisticated grunts.

The poorer one must outsmart the richer because his wits have been honed by his early struggle.

The greatest failing of the human species
is the desire to be led by the most
thuggish, narcissistic,
psychopath available.

Cheerful, unapologetic masculinity now held
to be toxic by the bien-pensant.

Facts don't care about your feelings.

Thank you for reading my book,

I do hope you enjoyed it.

Please post a short review on Amazon:

https://www.amazon.co.uk/review/create-review/listing

Your support really makes a difference.
I read all the reviews and value your feedback.

ravelston@seviourbooks.com

The drawings are by Kenny Bamgbose
Kennyvinci1@gmail.com
https://www.fiverr.com/share/7Xv7WL

Other books you might like:

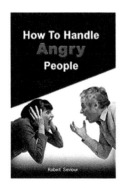

How to Handle Angry People:
A guide for people who may encounter aggression at work or in their personal life. How to cope with hostile, manipulative and difficult people and stay safe. You'll learn how to handle people with anger issues. Whether they are a threatening customer, a co-worker, a family member who is making your life stressful, you'll learn how best to deal with them.

A bit of a sore throat
A patient's perspective on throat cancer and its treatment. The author's personal experience of stage 4 throat cancer and what he learned by researching.

Hostel Hell

A real life story; the author's years of No Fixed Address spent with crooks, crazies, druggies, con men, prostitutes, streetwise survivors and a surprising number of really decent people.

An Amazon Books 'Best Seller' - 202 ratings

The Selling for Engineers manual:

How to win more profitable business.
A comprehensive guide to winning more good clients for your engineering, scientific or
technical company. Written by a sales engineer with 30 years of technical sales experience.